THE 30-MINUTE SHAKESPEARE

THE TEMPEST

"Nick Newlin's work as a teaching artist for Folger Education during the past thirteen years has provided students, regardless of their experience with Shakespeare or being on stage, a unique opportunity to tread the boards at the Folger Theatre. Working with students to edit Shakespeare's plays for performance at the annual Folger Shakespeare Festivals has enabled students to gain new insights into the Bard's plays, build their skills of comprehension and critical reading, and just plain have fun working collaboratively with their peers.

Folger Education promotes performance-based teaching of Shakespeare's plays, providing students with an interactive approach to Shakespeare's plays in which they participate in a close reading of the text through intellectual, physical, and vocal engagement. Newlin's *The 30-Minute Shakespeare* series is an invaluable resource for teachers of Shakespeare, and for all who are interested in performing the plays."

ROBERT YOUNG, PH.D.
DIRECTOR OF EDUCATION
FOLGER SHAKESPEARE LIBRARY

The Tempest: The 30-Minute Shakespeare
ISBN 978-1-935550-28-0
Adaptation, essays, and notes ©2018 by Nick Newlin

Cover design by Sarah Juckniess
Printed in the United States of America

Distributed by Consortium Book Sales & Distribution
www.cbsd.com

NICOLO WHIMSEY PRESS
www.30MinuteShakespeare.com

Art Director: Sarah Juckniess
Managing Editors: Katherine Little, Leah Gordon

The
TEMPEST

THE 30-MINUTE SHAKESPEARE

Written by WILLIAM SHAKESPEARE

Abridged AND Edited
by NICK NEWLIN

Nicolo Whimsey
Press

Brandywine, MD

To my grandmother
Louisa Lawrence Wood Foulke
("Tutu")

who shared her love
of music and drama

Special thanks to Joanne Flynn, Bill Newlin, Eliza Newlin Carney, William and Louisa Newlin, Michael Tolaydo, Hilary Kacser, Sarah Juckniess, Katherine Little, Eva Zimmerman, Leah Gordon, Tanya Tolchin, Frank Harris, Julie Schaper and all of Consortium, Leo Bowman and the students, faculty, and staff at Banneker Academic High School, and Robert Young Ph.D. and the Folger Shakespeare Library, especially the wonderful Education Department.

✳ TABLE OF CONTENTS

✳ NO EXPERIENCE NECESSARY

I was not a big "actor type" in high school, so if you weren't either, or if the young people you work with are not, then this book is for you. Whether or not you work with "actor types," you can use this book to stage a lively and captivating thirty-minute version of a Shakespeare play. No experience is necessary.

When I was about eleven years old, my parents took me to see Shakespeare's *Two Gentlemen of Verona*, which was being performed as a Broadway musical. I didn't comprehend every word I heard, but I was enthralled with the language, the characters, and the story, and I understood enough of it to follow along. From then on, I associated Shakespeare with *fun*.

Of course Shakespeare is fun. The Elizabethan audiences knew it, which is one reason he was so popular. It didn't matter that some of the language eluded them. The characters were passionate and vibrant, and their conflicts were compelling. Young people study Shakespeare in high school, but more often than not they read his work like a text book and then get quizzed on academic elements of the play, such as plot, theme, and vocabulary. These are all very interesting, but not nearly as interesting as standing up and performing a scene! It is through performance that the play comes alive and all its "academic" elements are revealed. There is nothing more satisfying to a student or teacher than the feeling of "owning" a Shakespeare play, and that can only come from performing it.

But Shakespeare's plays are often two or more hours long, making the performance of an entire play almost out of the question. One can perform a single scene, which is certainly a good start, but what about the story? What about the changes a character goes through as the play progresses? When school groups perform one scene unedited, or when they lump several plays together, the audience can get lost. This is why I have always preferred to tell the story of the play.

The 30-Minute Shakespeare gives students and teachers a chance to get up on their feet and act out a Shakespeare play in half an hour, using his language. The emphasis is on key scenes, with narrative bridges between scenes to keep the audience caught up on the action. The stage directions are built into this script so that young actors do not have to stand in one place; they can move and tell the story with their actions as well as their words. And it can all be done in a classroom during class time!

That is where this book was born: not in a research library, a graduate school lecture, a professional stage, or even an after-school drama club. All of the play cuttings in *The 30-Minute Shakespeare* were first rehearsed in a D.C. public high school English class, and performed successfully at the Folger Shakespeare Library's annual Secondary School Shakespeare Festival. The players were not necessarily "actor types." For many of them, this was their first performance in a play.

Something almost miraculous happens when students perform Shakespeare. They "get" it. By occupying the characters and speaking the words out loud, students gain a level of understanding and appreciation that is unachievable by simply reading the text. That is the magic of a performance-based method of learning Shakespeare, and this book makes the formerly daunting task of staging a Shakespeare play possible for anybody.

With *The 30-Minute Shakespeare* book series I hope to help teachers and students produce a Shakespeare play in a short amount of time, thus jump-starting the process of discovering the beauty, magic, and fun of the Bard. Plot, theme, and language reveal themselves through the performance of these half-hour play cuttings, and everybody involved receives the priceless gift of "owning" a piece of Shakespeare. The result is an experience that is fun and engaging, and one that we can all carry with us as we play out our own lives on the stages of the world.

NICK NEWLIN
Brandywine, MD
March 2010

CHARACTERS IN THE PLAY

The following is a list of characters that appear in this cutting of The Tempest.

For the full breakdown of characters, see Sample Program.

PROSPERO: Former Duke of Milan, now a magician on a Mediterranean island

SAILORS

MASTER OF THE SHIP

BOATSWAIN OF THE SHIP

ALONSO: King of Naples

SEBASTIAN: Alonso's brother

ANTONIO: Usurping Duke of Milan, and Prospero's brother

FERDINAND: Prince of Naples, and Alonso's son

GONZALO: Counselor to Alonso, and friend to Prospero

MIRANDA: Prospero's daughter

ARIEL: An airy spirit, servant to Prospero

CALIBAN: A savage inhabitant of the island, servant to Prospero

TRINCULO: Servant to Alonso

STEPHANO: Alonso's drunken butler

STRANGE SHAPES

DOGS

NARRATOR

✳ SCENE 1. (ACT I, SCENE I)

On a ship at sea.

STAGEHAND *sets stool upstage right.*

SOUND OPERATOR *plays* Sound Cue #1 ("Storm sounds").

Enter PROSPERO *from stage left. He stands on stool upstage right and "directs" the storm with his staff. Enter* SAILORS *from stage right, pulling ropes in slow motion as* NARRATOR *speaks.*

Enter NARRATOR *from stage rear, coming downstage center.*

NARRATOR
> On board a ship carrying King Alonso of Naples and his men, a boatswain directs the crew to fight a great storm *(raises voice over growing storm noises)* . . . but the ship appears destined to sink!

Exit NARRATOR *stage left. Exit* PROSPERO *and* SAILORS *stage right.*

Enter MASTER *and* BOATSWAIN *from stage right.*

MASTER
> Boatswain!

BOATSWAIN
> Here, master: What cheer?

MASTER

> Good, speak to the mariners: fall to't, yarely,
> or we run ourselves aground: bestir, bestir.

Exit MASTER *stage right.*

Enter SAILORS *from stage right, pulling on rope.*

BOATSWAIN

> Heigh, my hearts! Cheerly!
> Yare, yare! Take in the topsail!

Enter ALONSO, SEBASTIAN, ANTONIO, FERDINAND, *and* GONZALO *from stage right.*

ALONSO

> Good boatswain, have care. Where's the master?

BOATSWAIN

> I pray now, keep below.

ANTONIO

> Where is the master, boatswain?

BOATSWAIN

> You mar our labor: keep your cabins!

GONZALO

> Nay, good, be patient.

BOATSWAIN

> When the sea is. Hence! What cares these roarers
> for the name of king? To cabin: trouble us not.
> Out of our way, I say.

GONZALO *(aside to* ANTONIO *and* ALONSO)
> I have great comfort from this fellow: methinks he
> hath no drowning mark upon him.

Exit ALONSO, SEBASTIAN, ANTONIO, FERDINAND, *and* GONZALO
stage right.

SOUND OPERATOR *plays* Sound Cue #2 ("Thunder").

SAILORS *lurch stage left, pulling rope.*

BOATSWAIN
> Down with the topmast! Yare! Lower, lower!

Re-enter SEBASTIAN, ANTONIO, *and* GONZALO *from stage right.*

> Yet again! What do you here? Have you a mind
> to sink?

SEBASTIAN
> A pox o' your throat, you bawling, blasphemous,
> incharitable dog!

BOATSWAIN
> Work you then.

ANTONIO
> Hang, cur! Hang, you whoreson, insolent noisemaker!
> We are less afraid to be drowned than thou art.

SOUND OPERATOR *plays* Sound Cue #3 ("Thunder").

SAILORS *lurch far stage right, pulling rope.*

BOATSWAIN
> Lay her a-hold! What, must our mouths be cold?

ANTONIO

> We are merely cheated of our lives by drunkards:
> Let's all sink with the king.

Exit ANTONIO *and* SEBASTIAN *stage right.*

GONZALO

> Now would I give a thousand furlongs of sea for an
> acre of barren ground.

Exit ALL *stage right.*

✳ **SCENE 2.** (ACT I, SCENE II)

The island. Before PROSPERO'S *cell.*

STAGEHANDS *remove stool from upstage left and place chair downstage, just right of center.*

Enter NARRATOR *from stage rear, coming downstage center.*

NARRATOR
> Prospero, the former Duke of Milan, has been stranded on a barren island for twelve years with his daughter, Miranda. He explains to her that he used his magic to raise the recent storm, but no one was harmed. King Alonso's son, Ferdinand, falls instantly in love with Miranda, to Prospero's delight.

Exit NARRATOR *stage left.*

Enter PROSPERO *and* MIRANDA *from stage right.* MIRANDA *sits in chair.*

MIRANDA *(standing, looking over the audience to the sea)*
> If by your art, my dearest father, you have
> Put the wild waters in this roar, allay them.
> A brave vessel, dash'd all to pieces.

PROSPERO
> Be collected: There's no harm done.
> I should inform thee farther. Pluck my magic
>   garment from me.
> *(lays down his mantle)*

Thou must now know farther.
Twelve year since, Miranda,
Thy father was the Duke of Milan.

MIRANDA

O the heavens!

PROSPERO

Thy uncle, call'd Antonio, did believe he was indeed
    the duke;
The King of Naples and Antonio prepared a rotten
    carcass of a boat;
There they hoist us, to cry to the sea that roar'd
    to us.

MIRANDA

How came we ashore?

PROSPERO

By Providence divine.
(dons his mantle again)

MIRANDA

I pray you, sir, your reason for raising this sea-storm?

PROSPERO

By accident most strange hath mine enemies
brought to this shore. Here cease more questions:
Thou art inclined to sleep.

PROSPERO *waves his hands, casting a spell over* **MIRANDA**.

SOUND OPERATOR *plays* Sound Cue #4 ("Ding").

MIRANDA *sleeps.*

Come, servant.
Approach, my Ariel, come.

Enter ARIEL *from stage right, playing the recorder.*

ARIEL

    All hail, great master! I come to answer thy
        best pleasure;
    To ride on the curl'd clouds,
    Ariel and all her quality.

PROSPERO

    Hast thou, spirit,
    Perform'd to point the tempest that I bade thee?

ARIEL

    To every article.
    I boarded the king's ship; I flamed amazement.
    The king's son, Ferdinand, was the first man
        that leap'd,
    Not a hair perish'd;
    In troops I have dispersed them 'bout the isle.
    The king's son have I landed by himself.

PROSPERO

    Ariel, there's more work.

ARIEL

    Is there more toil?
    Let me remember thee what thou hast promised,
    My liberty.

PROSPERO

    Do so, and after two days
    I will discharge thee.
    Go make thyself invisible.

Exit ARIEL *stage right.*

SOUND OPERATOR *plays* Sound Cue #5 ("Ding").

> *(to* MIRANDA*)* Awake, dear heart, awake! Thou hast
> slept well; awake!

MIRANDA *awakes.*

Re-enter ARIEL *from stage right, invisible, playing and singing,*
with FERDINAND *following.*

FERDINAND
> Where should this music be? I' the air or the earth?

ARIEL
> Full fathom five thy father lies;
> Those are pearls that were his eyes.

FERDINAND *(agitated, sad)*
> The ditty does remember my drown'd father.

MIRANDA
> What is't? A spirit? It carries a brave form.
> I might call her a thing divine.

PROSPERO *(aside to* ARIEL*)*
> It goes on, I see,
> As my soul prompts it.

ARIEL, *still invisible, turns* FERDINAND *around to face* MIRANDA.

FERDINAND
> My prime request is, O you wonder! If you be
>   maid or no?

MIRANDA
> No wonder, sir; but certainly a maid.

PROSPERO *(aside)*
> They are both in either's powers.

SOUND OPERATOR *plays* Sound Cue #6 ("Ding").

MIRANDA *freezes.*

FERDINAND
> My father's loss, the wreck of all my friends, are but
>> light to me,
> Might I but through my prison once a day
> Behold this maid.

PROSPERO *(aside)*
> It works.

SOUND OPERATOR *plays* Sound Cue #7 ("Ding").

FERDINAND *freezes.*

> *(to* **ARIEL***)* Thou hast done well, fine Ariel!
> Thou shalt be free
> As mountain winds: but then exactly do
> All points of my command.

ARIEL
> To the syllable.

SOUND OPERATOR *plays* Sound Cue #8 ("Ding").

MIRANDA *and* **FERDINAND** *are unfrozen.*

PROSPERO *(sternly)*
> Come, follow.

Exit **ALL** *stage right.*

✳ SCENE 3. (ACT II, SCENE II)

Another part of the island.

Enter NARRATOR *from stage rear, coming downstage center.*

NARRATOR
>Having escaped the apparently sinking ship,
>Trinculo hides under a cloak to weather the storm,
>where he discovers the island's ornery monster,
>Caliban. Drunk Stephano finds them both and
>shares his bottle with them, which livens things up!

Exit NARRATOR *stage left.*

Enter CALIBAN *from stage right, carrying a bundle of wood.*

SOUND OPERATOR *plays* Sound Cue #9 ("Thunder").

CALIBAN
>All the infections that the sun sucks up
>From bogs on Prosper fall.

Enter TRINCULO *from stage right.*

>Lo, now, lo!
>Here comes a spirit of his. I'll fall flat.
>>*(hides under his cloak)*

TRINCULO
>Another storm brewing;
>I know not where to hide my head:
>What have we here? A man or a fish? Dead or alive?

> *(lifts up the cloak)*
> A fish: he smells like a fish.
> A strange fish! Legged like a man *(noticing*
> CALIBAN'S *arms)* and his fins like arms!
> Warm o' my troth!

SOUND OPERATOR *plays* Sound Cue #10 ("Thunder").

TRINCULO *panics at the sounds of the storm.*

> Alas, the storm is come again! My best way is to
> creep under his gaberdine.

TRINCULO *holds his nose to block the smell and crawls under the cloak.* CALIBAN *immediately sticks his head out from under the cloak with a startled look.*

Enter STEPHANO *from stage left, singing, with a flask in his hand.*

STEPHANO
> I shall no more to sea, to sea,
> Here shall I die ashore—*(drinks)*
> This is a scurvy tune too: but here's my comfort.
> *(drinks)*

CALIBAN *(frightened by* STEPHANO'S *singing and arrival)*
> Do not torment me: oh!

STEPHANO *jumps at the sound and notices the four legs sticking out from under the cloak.*

STEPHANO
> I have not scaped drowning to be afeard now of your
> *(counting)* four legs.

CALIBAN
> Do not torment me, prithee.

STEPHANO

He's in his fit now. He shall taste of my bottle:
Open your mouth.

STEPHANO *passes flask to* CALIBAN, *who takes a few long swigs with large breaths between sips.*

TRINCULO

I should know that voice: it should be—but he
is drowned.

STEPHANO

Four legs and two voices: a most delicate monster!
I will pour some in thy other mouth. (*moves to pour
drink on* TRINCULO'S *side of the cloak*)

TRINCULO

Stephano!

STEPHANO *shrieks.*

Stephano! I am Trinculo—be not afeard—
thy good friend (*emerges from cloak, revealing
himself*) Trinculo.

STEPHANO

I'll pull thee by the lesser legs.

STEPHANO *pulls* TRINCULO *by his legs;* TRINCULO *protests
when pulled.*

Thou art very Trinculo indeed! How camest
thou to be the siege of this moon-calf? Can he
vent Trinculos?

TRINCULO

But art thou not drowned, Stephano?

STEPHANO *shakes his head.*

> O Stephano, two Neapolitans 'scaped!

TRINCULO *grabs* STEPHANO *as they dance around in a circle.*

STEPHANO
> Prithee, do not turn me about; my stomach is
> not constant.

CALIBAN *(aside)*
> That's a brave god and bears celestial liquor.
> I will kneel to him. *(kneels)*

STEPHANO
> How didst thou 'scape?

TRINCULO
> Swum ashore. Man, like a duck.

STEPHANO
> Here, kiss the book.

STEPHANO *hands flask to* CALIBAN, *who drinks greedily.*

CALIBAN
> I'll kiss thy foot; I'll swear myself thy subject.
> I'll fish for thee and get thee wood enough.
> A plague upon the tyrant that I serve!
> I'll follow thee, thou wondrous man.
> > *(singing drunkenly)*
> Farewell master; farewell, farewell!

TRINCULO
> A howling monster: a drunken monster!

CALIBAN
> 'Ban, 'Ban, Ca-caliban
> Has a new master: get a new man.
> Freedom, hie-day! Hie-day, freedom!

STEPHANO
> O brave monster! Lead the way.

Exit **ALL** *stage left, singing* **CALIBAN'S** *song and dancing merrily.*

✳ **SCENE 4.** (ACT III, SCENE I)

Before **PROSPERO'S** *cell.*

STAGEHAND *places stool stage right.*

Enter **NARRATOR** *from stage rear, coming downstage center.*

NARRATOR
>Ferdinand is visited by Miranda. Prospero observes
>them, unseen, as they exchange marriage vows.
>Things are starting to heat up!

Exit **NARRATOR** *stage left.*

Enter **FERDINAND** *from stage right, picking up logs.*

FERDINAND
>This my mean task would be heavy to me, but
>The mistress which I serve quickens what's dead
>And makes my labors pleasures.

Enter **MIRANDA** *from stage right.* **PROSPERO** *follows; he lingers upstage, unseen.*

MIRANDA *sits.* **PROSPERO** *continues to hang back, upstage right. Upon seeing* **MIRANDA,** **FERDINAND** *drops a log from his bundle.*

MIRANDA
>Work not so hard: rest yourself;

MIRANDA *takes* **FERDINAND** *by the hand, leading him gently to the stool.*

I'll bear your logs the while.

MIRANDA *pretends to struggle to pick up a log, looking over at* FERDINAND. FERDINAND *gently leads* MIRANDA *back to the stool while speaking, kneeling as she sits.*

FERDINAND
No, precious creature;
I had rather break my back,
Than you should such dishonor undergo,
While I sit lazy by.

PROSPERO
Poor worm, thou art infected!

FERDINAND
What is your name?

MIRANDA
Miranda.—O my father,
I have broke your hest to say so!

FERDINAND
Admired Miranda!
O you are created of every creature's best!

MIRANDA
How features are abroad,
I am skilless of. I would not wish
Any companion in the world but you.

MIRANDA *takes* FERDINAND'S *arm.*

FERDINAND
The very instant that I saw you, did
My heart fly to your service;

And for your sake am I this patient *(pauses, gesturing to logs)* log-man.

MIRANDA

Do you love me?

FERDINAND

I beyond all limit of what else i' the world
Do love, prize, honor you.

MIRANDA

I am a fool
To weep at what I am glad of.

PROSPERO

Fair encounter
Of two most rare affections!

MIRANDA

I am your wife, if you will marry me.

FERDINAND

Ay, with a heart as willing
As bondage e'er of freedom: here's my hand.

MIRANDA

And mine, with my heart in't; and now farewell.

FERDINAND

A thousand thousand!

Exit FERDINAND *and* MIRANDA *stage left.*

PROSPERO

So glad of this as they I cannot be,
Who are surprised withal; but my rejoicing

At nothing can be more. I'll to my book,
For yet ere supper-time must I perform
Much business appertaining.

Exit **PROSPERO** *stage left.*

✳ **SCENE 5.** (ACT III, SCENE II)

Another part of the island.

Enter **NARRATOR** *from stage rear, coming downstage center.*

NARRATOR
> Trinculo and Caliban quarrel with the help of the
> invisible fairy Ariel. Caliban urges Stephano to kill
> Prospero. What a monstrous thing to do!

Exit **NARRATOR** *stage left.*

Enter **CALIBAN**, **STEPHANO**, *and* **TRINCULO** *from stage right,*
drinking and carousing. They stand downstage from stool.

STEPHANO
> Servant-monster, drink to me.

STEPHANO *hands a drink to* **CALIBAN**, *who takes a long gulp.*
TRINCULO *is not happy with this.*

CALIBAN
> Let me lick thy shoe. *(kneels on floor)*
> I thank my noble lord.

Enter **ARIEL** *from stage right, invisible to all. She stands on stool.*

CALIBAN
> As I told thee before, I am subject to a tyrant,
> a sorcerer, that by his cunning hath cheated me of
> the island.

ARIEL

Thou liest.

CALIBAN *(to* **TRINCULO***)*

Thou liest, thou jesting monkey, thou! I do not lie.

STEPHANO

Trinculo, if you trouble him any more, I will
supplant some of your teeth.

TRINCULO

I did nothing.

STEPHANO

Didst thou not say he lied?

ARIEL

Thou liest.

STEPHANO

Do I so? Take thou that.
(beats **TRINCULO** *with his hat)*
Proceed.

CALIBAN *(conspiratorially, pulling* **STEPHANO** *closer)*

Why, as I told thee, 'tis a custom with Prospero
I' th' afternoon to sleep: there thou mayst brain him,
With a log or cut his wezand with thy knife.
Remember first to possess his books; for without them
He's but a sot, as I am, nor hath not
One spirit to command:
And that most deeply to consider is
The beauty of his daughter;
She will become thy bed,
And bring thee forth brave brood.

STEPHANO

> Monster, I will kill this man: his daughter and I will
> be king and queen—save our graces!—and Trinculo
> and thyself shall be viceroys. Come on, Trinculo, let
> us sing.
>> *(singing)*
>
> Flout 'em and scout 'em
> And scout 'em and flout 'em
> Thought is free.

ALL *sing the song together, happily dancing as they start to exit.*
ARIEL *plays the tune on a recorder.*

CALIBAN

> Be not afeard; the isle is full of noises,
> That give delight and hurt not.

STEPHANO

> This will prove a brave kingdom to me, where I shall
> have my music for nothing. Lead, monster; we'll
> follow.

Exit ALL *stage right.*

✳ SCENE 6. (ACT III, SCENE III)

Another part of the island.

STAGEHANDS *set banquet table upstage center and place stool center stage. They place second stool upstage left.*

Enter NARRATOR *from stage rear, coming downstage center.*

NARRATOR

>King Alonso and his party are visited by strange shapes that invite them to a banquet. Ariel appears as a large winged bird called a harpy and accuses three of the men of overthrowing Prospero's dukedom, threatening them with a fate worse than death. Rule number one: Never mess with a harpy!

Exit NARRATOR *stage left.*

Enter ALONSO, SEBASTIAN, ANTONIO, *and* GONZALO *from stage left.*

GONZALO

>I can go no further, sir. My old bones ache.

ALONSO

>Sit down, and rest.

GONZALO *sits on floor, stage right;* ALONSO *sits on stool center stage.*

>Even here I will put off my hope; he is drown'd
>Whom thus we stray to find. Well, let him go.

ANTONIO *(standing stage left with* **SEBASTIAN***)*
> *(aside to* **SEBASTIAN***)* I am right glad that he's so out
> of hope.

SEBASTIAN *(aside to* **ANTONIO***)*
> The next advantage will we take throughly.

ANTONIO
> *(aside to* **SEBASTIAN***)* Let it be tonight.

SOUND OPERATOR *plays* Sound Cue #11 ("Strange shapes music").

ALONSO
> What harmony is this?

GONZALO
> Marvelous sweet music!

Enter **PROSPERO** *from stage rear. He stands on upstage left stool, invisible to all. Enter several* **STRANGE SHAPES** *from stage rear. They move gracefully around the stage, dancing about the banquet table with gentle actions. After inviting* **ALONSO**, **ANTONIO**, *and* **SEBASTIAN** *to eat,* **STRANGE SHAPES** *depart.*

SEBASTIAN
> Now I will believe
> That there are unicorns.

GONZALO
> If in Naples
> I should report this now, would they believe me?

ALONSO
> I will stand to and feed.

SOUND OPERATOR *plays* Sound Cue #12 ("Thunder").

Enter ARIEL, *as Harpy, from stage left. She stands on center stage stool.*

ARIEL
> You are three men of sin, whom Destiny,
> Hath caused to belch up you; I have made you mad.

ALONSO, SEBASTIAN, *and* ANTONIO *draw their swords.*

SOUND OPERATOR *plays* Sound Cue #13 ("Ding").

> You fools! Your swords may as well
> Wound the loud winds, or
> Kill the still-closing waters.

SOUND OPERATOR *plays* Sound Cue #14 ("Ding").

> You three
> From Milan did supplant good Prospero;
> Exposed unto the sea,
> Him and his innocent child.
> *(to* ALONSO*)* Thee of thy son, Alonso,
> They have bereft; and do pronounce by me:
> Lingering perdition.

SOUND OPERATOR *plays* Sound Cue #15 ("Thunder").

SOUND OPERATOR *plays* Sound Cue #16 ("Strange and solemn music").

Re-enter STRANGE SHAPES, *dancing, from stage rear.* PROSPERO *follows, unseen, and stands on upstage left stool to observe.*

ARIEL, *as Harpy, descends from stool, removes bird mask, and moves upstage left to stand with Prospero.*

Exit STRANGE SHAPES *stage left.*

PROSPERO

> Bravely the figure of this harpy hast thou
> Perform'd, my Ariel. My high charms work
> And these mine enemies now are in my power.

Exit ARIEL *and* PROSPERO *stage left.*

ALONSO

> O, it is monstrous, monstrous.

Exit ALONSO, SEBASTIAN, *and* ANTONIO *stage right.*

GONZALO

> All three of them are desperate: their great guilt,
> Like poison now 'gins to bite the spirits.

Exit GONZALO *stage right.*

STAGEHANDS *remove banquet table.*

✳ **SCENE 7.** (ACT IV, SCENE I)

Before **PROSPERO'S** *cell.*

Enter **NARRATOR** *from stage rear, coming downstage center.*

NARRATOR
> Prospero gives his daughter's hand to Ferdinand and the couple are married. He suddenly remembers the threat posed by Caliban and company and drives them out with spirits disguised as dogs. Rule number two: Never mess with a magician.

Exit **NARRATOR** *stage left.*

Enter **PROSPERO, FERDINAND,** *and* **MIRANDA** *from stage right.*

PROSPERO
> Take my daughter.

FERDINAND
> I hope for quiet days, fair issue and long life.

PROSPERO
> What, Ariel! My industrious servant, Ariel!

Enter **ARIEL,** *humming, from stage right.*

ARIEL
> Here I am.

PROSPERO

      I must use you in such another trick. Go bring
          the rabble,
      O'er whom I give thee power, here to this place.

ARIEL

      Before you can say 'come' and 'go,'
      Each one, tripping on his toe,
      Will be here with mop and mow.
      Do you love me, master? No?

PROSPERO

      Dearly my delicate Ariel.

Exit ARIEL, *humming, stage left.*

PROSPERO *(aside, suddenly very angry)*

      I had forgot that foul conspiracy
      Of the beast Caliban and his confederates
      Against my life: the minute of their plot
      Is almost come.

FERDINAND

      This is strange: your father's in some passion
      That works him strongly.

MIRANDA

      Never till this day
      Saw I him touch'd with anger so distemper'd.

PROSPERO

      My brain is troubled.

FERDINAND

      We wish your peace.

Exit FERDINAND *and* MIRANDA *stage right.*

PROSPERO
>Ariel: come.

Enter ARIEL *from stage left.*

ARIEL
>What's thy pleasure?

PROSPERO
>Spirit,
>We must prepare to meet with Caliban.
>Where didst thou leave these varlets?

ARIEL
>*(gestures offstage, miming a pool)*
>I left them i' the filthy-mantled pool beyond your
>cell.

PROSPERO
>This was well done, my bird.
>Thy shape invisible retain thou still.

SOUND OPERATOR *plays* Sound Cue #17 ("Ding").

ARIEL *(twitching nose)*
>I go, I go.

Exit ARIEL *stage left.*

PROSPERO
>I will plague them all, even to roaring.

Enter CALIBAN, STEPHANO, *and* TRINCULO, *each wet from the pool, from stage right.* PROSPERO *and* ARIEL *remain invisible.*

CALIBAN *(gesturing for* STEPHANO *and* TRINCULO *to follow)*
(whispering loudly) Pray you, tread softly.

TRINCULO
Monster, I do smell all horse-piss;
at which my nose is in great indignation.

STEPHANO
So is mine.

CALIBAN
Be patient, my king, be quiet.
This is the mouth o' the cell:
Do that good mischief which may make this island
Thine own for ever, and I, thy Caliban,
Thy foot-licker.

PROSPERO *gestures toward offstage. Enter* DOG ONE *from stage rear.* DOG ONE *starts after* TRINCULO, *who runs away and hops on stool, afraid, trying to kick* DOG ONE *away with his feet.*

PROSPERO
Hey, Mountain, hey!

ARIEL *gestures toward offstage. Enter* DOG TWO *from stage rear.* DOG TWO *starts after* CALIBAN, *who growls and bears his teeth;* DOG TWO *growls and bears his teeth back.*

ARIEL
Silver I there it goes, Silver!

PROSPERO
Fury, fury! There, there! Hark! Hark!

Enter DOG THREE *from stage rear.* DOG THREE *starts after* STEPHANO *and chases him around the stage.*

Exit TRINCULO, CALIBAN, *and* STEPHANO *stage right, pursued by* DOGS.

ARIEL *(laughing hysterically)*
   Hark, they roar!

PROSPERO *(laughs merrily, then becomes serious)*
    Let them be hunted soundly. At this hour
    Lie at my mercy all mine enemies:
    Follow, and do me service.

Exit PROSPERO *and* ARIEL *stage right.*

✳ **SCENE 8.** (ACT V, SCENE I)

Before **PROSPERO'S** *cell.*

Enter **NARRATOR** *from stage rear, coming downstage center.*

NARRATOR

> Prospero releases Alonso and his party from their
> charmed state and renounces the further use of
> his magic. Prospero's dukedom is restored, all is
> forgiven, and family members are reunited. Almost
> everyone is well on the way to being free! This must
> be a Shakespearean comedy!

Exit **NARRATOR** *stage left.*

Enter **PROSPERO**, *in his magician's robes, and* **ARIEL** *from
stage right.*

PROSPERO

> Now does my project gather to a head:
> My charms crack not; my spirits obey.
> How fares the king and his followers?

ARIEL

> Just as you left them; all prisoners, sir,
> Gonzalo's tears run down his beard, like winter's drops
> From eaves of reeds.

PROSPERO

> I am struck to the quick,
> The rarer action is

> In virtue than in vengeance:
> Go release them, Ariel:
> My charms I'll break.

ARIEL

> I'll fetch them, sir.

Exit ARIEL *stage right.*

PROSPERO

> I have bedimm'd
> The noontide sun, call'd forth the mutinous winds,
> And 'twixt the green sea and the azured vault
> Set roaring war: but this rough magic
> I here abjure, I'll break my staff,
> I'll drown my book.

SOUND OPERATOR *plays* Sound Cue #18 ("Hypnotic music").

Re-enter ARIEL *from stage right.* ALONSO *follows, attended by* GONZALO, SEBASTIAN, *and* ANTONIO. *As* PROSPERO *"conducts" their movements,* ALL *walk around the stage in a circle, ending by forming a semicircle that faces the audience. They stand, charmed.*

SOUND OPERATOR *plays* Sound Cue #19 ("Ding").

ALL *unfreeze.*

> There stand,
> For you are spell-stopp'd.
> Most cruelly didst thou, Alonso, use me and
>   my daughter:
> Thy brother was a furtherer in the act,
> Would here have kill'd your king;
> Quickly, spirit; thou shalt ere long be free.

ARIEL *(singing)*
> Merrily, merrily shall I live now
> Under the blossom that hangs on the bough.

PROSPERO
> My dainty Ariel! To the king's ship,
> There shalt thou find the master and the boatswain.
> Enforce them to this place, presently.

ARIEL
> I drink the air before me, and return.

SOUND OPERATOR *plays* Sound Cue #20 ("Ding").

Exit **ARIEL** *stage left.*

PROSPERO *(to* **ALONSO***)*
> Behold, sir king,
> The wronged Duke of Milan, Prospero.

ALONSO
> Thy pulse
> Beats as of flesh and blood; and, since I saw thee,
> The affliction of my mind amends,
> Thy dukedom I resign and do entreat
> Thou pardon me my wrongs.

PROSPERO *(aside to* **SEBASTIAN** *and* **ANTONIO***)*
> But you, my brace of lords, were I so minded,
> I here could justify you traitors.

SEBASTIAN *(aside)*
> The devil speaks in him.

PROSPERO *(to* **ANTONIO***)*
> No. For you, most wicked sir, I do forgive
> Thy rankest fault.

ALONSO

> I have lost my dear son Ferdinand.

PROSPERO

> I have lost my daughter.
> I will requite you with as good a thing.

Enter FERDINAND *and* MIRANDA *from stage left.* ALONSO *is astonished and joyful to see his son alive.*

ALONSO

> If this prove
> A vision of the Island, one dear son
> Shall I twice lose.

SEBASTIAN

> A most high miracle!

FERDINAND (*to* ALONSO)

> Though the seas threaten, they are merciful;
> I have cursed them without cause.
> > (*kneels*)

MIRANDA (*looking at men with amazement and attraction*)
> O, wonder!
> How many goodly creatures are there here!
> How beauteous mankind is! O brave new world,
> That has such people in't!

PROSPERO

> 'Tis new to thee.

ALONSO

> Is she the goddess that hath sever'd us,
> And brought us thus together?

FERDINAND
>Sir, she is mortal;
>But by immortal Providence she's mine:
>She is daughter to this famous Duke of Milan,
>And second father this lady makes him to me.

ALONSO
>I am hers:
>*(to* MIRANDA*)* I must ask my child forgiveness!
>*(to* FERDINAND *and* MIRANDA*)* Give me your hands.

GONZALO
>Be it so! Amen!

Re-enter ARIEL *from stage left, with* MASTER *and* BOATSWAIN *following in amazement.*

>What is the news?

BOATSWAIN
>We have safely found
>Our king and company. Our ship—
>Which we gave out split—
>Is tight and yare and bravely rigg'd as when
>We first put out to sea.

PROSPERO *(aside to* ARIEL*)*
>My tricksy spirit!
>Thou shalt be free.
>Set Caliban and his companions free;
>Untie the spell.

Exit ARIEL *stage left.*

PROSPERO *(to* ALONSO*)*

How fares my gracious sir?
There are yet missing of your company.

Re-enter ARIEL *from stage left, driving in* CALIBAN, STEPHANO, *and* TRINCULO.

SEBASTIAN

Ha, ha!
What things are these, my lord Antonio?
Will money buy 'em?

ANTONIO

One of them
Is a plain fish, and, no doubt, marketable.

PROSPERO

This misshapen demi-devil
had plotted with them to take my life.

CALIBAN

I shall be pinch'd to death.

ALONSO

Is not this Stephano, my drunken butler?
And Trinculo is reeling ripe:
How camest thou in this pickle?

TRINCULO

I have been in such a pickle since I
saw you last.

SEBASTIAN

How now, Stephano!

STEPHANO
> I am not Stephano, but a cramp.

PROSPERO *(pointing to* **CALIBAN***)*
> Go, sirrah, to my cell.

CALIBAN
> Ay, that I will; what a thrice-double ass
> Was I, to take this drunkard for a god
> And worship this dull fool!

Exit **CALIBAN**, **STEPHANO**, *and* **TRINCULO** *stage left.*

PROSPERO
> Your highness; in the morn
> I'll bring you to your ship;
> And thence retire me to my Milan, where
> Every third thought shall be my grave.

ALONSO
> I long
> To hear the story of your life, which must
> Take the ear strangely.

PROSPERO
> I'll deliver all;
> And promise you calm seas, auspicious gales.
> *(aside to* **ARIEL***)* My Ariel, chick,
> To the elements be free, and fare thou well!

Exit **ARIEL** *stage left.*

PROSPERO
> Now my charms are all o'erthrown,
> And what strength I have's mine own,
> But release me from my bands

>With the help of your good hands:
>As you from crimes would pardon'd be,
>Let your indulgence set me free.

Re-enter **ALL** *from stage left.*

ALL

>Our revels now are ended. These our actors,
>Were all spirits and
>Are melted into air, into thin air:
>We are such stuff
>As dreams are made on, and our little life
>Is rounded with a sleep.

ALL *hold hands and take a bow. Exeunt.*

✳ PERFORMING SHAKESPEARE

HOW *THE 30-MINUTE SHAKESPEARE* WAS BORN

In 1981 I performed a "Shakespeare Juggling" piece called "To Juggle or Not To Juggle" at the first Folger Library Secondary School Shakespeare Festival. The audience consisted of about 200 Washington, D.C. area high school students who had just performed thirty-minute versions of Shakespeare plays for each other and were jubilant over the experience. I was dressed in a jester's outfit, and my job was to entertain them. I juggled and jested and played with Shakespeare's words, notably Hamlet's "To be or not to be" soliloquy, to very enthusiastic response. I was struck by how much my "Shakespeare Juggling" resonated with a group who had just performed Shakespeare themselves. "Getting" Shakespeare is a heady feeling, especially for adolescents, and I am continually delighted at how much joy and satisfaction young people derive from performing Shakespeare. Simply reading and studying this great playwright does not even come close to inspiring the kind of enthusiasm that comes from performance.

Surprisingly, many of these students were not "actor types." A good percentage of the students performing Shakespeare that day were part of an English class which had rehearsed the plays during class time. Fifteen years later, when I first started directing plays in D.C. public schools as a Teaching Artist with the Folger Shakespeare Library, I entered a ninth grade English class as a guest and spent two or three days a week for two or three months preparing students for the Folger's annual Secondary School Shakespeare Festival. I have conducted this annual residency with the Folger ever since. Every year for seven action-packed days, eight groups of students between grades seven and twelve tread the boards onstage at the Folger's Elizabethan Theatre, a grand recreation of a sixteenth-century venue with a three-tiered gallery, carved oak columns, and a sky-painted canopy.

As noted on the Folger website (www.folger.edu), "The festival is a celebration of the Bard, not a competition. Festival commentators—drawn from the professional theater and Shakespeare education communities—recognize exceptional performances, student directors, and good spirit amongst the students with selected awards at the end of each day. They are also available to share feedback with the students."

My annual Folger Teaching Artist engagement, directing a Shakespeare play in a public high school English class, is the most challenging and the most rewarding thing I do all year. I hope this book can bring you the same rewards.

GETTING STARTED

GAMES

How can you get an English class (or any other group of young people, or even adults) to start the seemingly daunting task of performing a Shakespeare play? You have already successfully completed the critical first step, which is buying this book. You hold in your hand a performance-ready, thirty-minute cutting of a Shakespeare play, with stage directions to get the actors moving about the stage purposefully. But it's a good idea to warm the group up with some theater games.

One good initial exercise is called "Positive/Negative Salutations." Students stand in two lines facing each other (four or five students in each line) and, reading from index cards, greet each other, first with a "Positive" salutation in Shakespeare's language (using actual phrases from the plays), followed by a "negative" greeting.

Additionally, short vocal exercises are an essential part of the preparation process. The following is a very simple and effective vocal warm-up: Beginning with the number two, have the whole group count to twenty using increments of two (i.e., "Two, four, six . . ."). Increase the volume slightly with each number, reaching top volume with "twenty," and then decrease the volume while counting back down, so that the students are practically whispering when they arrive again at "two." This exercise teaches dynamics and allows them to get loud as a group without any individual pressure. Frequently during a rehearsal period, if a student is mumbling inaudibly, I will refer back to this exercise as a reminder that we can and often do belt it out!

"Stomping Words" is a game that is very helpful at getting a handle on Shakespeare's rhythm. Choose a passage in iambic pentameter and have the group members walk around the room in a circle, stomping their feet on the second beat of each line:

Two **house**-holds, **both** a-**like** in **dig**-nity
In **fair** Ve-**ro**na **Where** we **lay** our **scene**

Do the same thing with a prose passage, and have the students discuss their experience with it, including points at which there is an extra beat, etc., and what, if anything, it might signify.

I end every vocal warm-up with a group reading of one of the speeches from the play, emphasizing diction and projection, bouncing off consonants, and encouraging the group members to listen to each other so that they can speak the lines together in unison. For variety I will throw in some classic "tongue twisters" too, such as, "The sixth sheik's sixth sheep is sick."

The Folger Shakespeare Library's website (http://www.folger.edu) and their book series *Shakespeare Set Free,* edited by Peggy O'Brien, are two great resources for getting started with a performance-based teaching of Shakespeare in the classroom. The Folger website has numerous helpful resources and activities, many submitted by teachers, for helping a class actively participate in the process of getting to know a Shakespeare play. For more simple theater games, Viola Spolin's *Theatre Games for the Classroom* is very helpful, as is one I use frequently, *Theatre Games for Young Performers.*

HATS AND PROPS

Introducing a few hats and props early in the process is a good way to get the action going. Hats, in particular, provide a nice avenue for giving young actors a non-verbal way of getting into character. In the opening weeks, when students are still holding onto their scripts, a hat can give an actor a way to "feel" like a character. Young actors are natural masters at injecting their own personality into what they wear, and even small choices made with how a hat is worn (jauntily, shadily, cockily, mysteriously) provide a starting point for discussion of specific characters, their traits, and their relationships with other characters. All such discussions always lead back to one thing: the text. "Mining the text" is consistently the best strategy for uncovering the mystery of Shakespeare's language. That is where all the answers lie: in the words themselves.

WHAT DO THE WORDS MEAN?

It is essential that young actors know what they are saying when they recite Shakespeare. If not, they might as well be scat singing, riffing on sounds and rhythm but not conveying a specific meaning. The real question is: What do the words mean? The answer is multifaceted, and can be found in more than one place. The New Folger Library paperback editions of the plays themselves (edited by Barbara Mowat and Paul Werstine, Washington Square Press) are a great resource for understanding Shakespeare's words and passages and "translating" them into modern English. These editions also contain chapters on Shakespeare's language, his life, his theater, a "Modern Perspective," and further reading. There is a wealth of scholarship embedded in these wonderful books, and I make it a point to read them cover to cover before embarking on a play-directing project. At the very least, it is a good idea for any adult who intends to direct a Shakespeare play with a group of students to go through the explanatory notes that appear on the pages facing the text. These explanatory notes are an indispensable "translation tool."

The best way to get students to understand what Shakespeare's words mean is to ask them what they think they mean. Students have their own associations with the words and with how they sound and feel. The best ideas on how to perform Shakespeare often come directly from the students, not from anybody else's notion. If a student has an idea or feeling about a word or passage, and it resonates with her emotionally, physically, or spiritually, then Shakespeare's words can be a vehicle for her feelings. That can result in some powerful performances!

I make it my job as director to read the explanatory notes in the Folger text, but I make it clear to the students that almost "anything goes" when trying to understand Shakespeare. There are no wrong interpretations. Students have their own experiences, with some shared and some uniquely their own. If someone has an association with the phrase "canker-blossom," or if the words make that student or his character feel or act a certain way, then that is the "right" way to decipher it.

I encourage the students to refer to the Folger text's explanatory notes and to keep a pocket dictionary handy. Young actors must attach some meaning to every word or line they recite. If I feel an actor is glossing over a word, I will stop him and ask him what he is saying. If he doesn't know, we will figure it out together as a group.

PROCESS VS. PRODUCT

The process of learning Shakespeare by performing one of his plays is more important than whether everybody remembers his lines or whether somebody misses a cue or an entrance. But my Teaching Artist residencies have always had the end goal of a public performance for about 200 other students, so naturally the performance starts to take precedence over the process somewhere around dress rehearsal in the students' minds. It is my job to make sure the actors are prepared—otherwise they will remember the embarrassing moment of a public mistake and not the glorious triumph of owning a Shakespeare play.

In one of my earlier years of play directing, I was sitting in the audience as one of my narrators stood frozen on stage for at least a minute, trying to remember her opening line. I started scrambling in my backpack below my seat for a script, at last prompting her from the audience. Despite her fine performance, that embarrassing moment is all she remembered from the whole experience. Since then I have made sure to assign at least one person to prompt from backstage if necessary. Additionally, I inform the entire cast that if somebody is dying alone out there, it is okay to rescue him or her with an offstage prompt.

There is always a certain amount of stage fright that will accompany a performance, especially a public one for an unfamiliar audience. As a director, I live with stage fright as well, even though I am not appearing on stage. The only antidote to this is work and preparation. If a young actor is struggling with her lines, I make sure to arrange for a session where we run lines over the telephone. I try to set up a buddy system so that students can run lines with their peers, and this often works well. But if somebody does not have a "buddy," I will personally make the time to help out myself. As I assure my students from the outset, I am not going to let them fail or embarrass themselves. They need an experienced leader. And if the leader has experience in teaching but not in directing Shakespeare, then he needs this book!

It is a good idea to culminate in a public performance, as opposed to an in-class project, even if it is only for another classroom. Student actors want to show their newfound Shakespearian thespian skills to an outside group, and this goal motivates them to do a good job. In that respect, "product" is important. Another wonderful bonus to performing a play is that it is a unifying group effort. Students learn teamwork. They learn to give focus to another actor when he is speaking, and to play off of other characters. I like to end each performance with the entire cast reciting a passage in unison. This is a powerful ending, one that reaffirms the unity of the group.

SEEING SHAKESPEARE PERFORMED

It is very helpful for young actors to see Shakespeare performed by a group of professionals, whether they are appearing live on stage (preferable but not always possible) or on film. Because an entire play can take up two or more full class periods, time may be an issue. I am fortunate because thanks to a local foundation that underwrites theater education in the schools, I have been able to take my school groups to a Folger Theatre matinee of the play that they are performing. I always pick a play that is being performed locally that season. But not all group leaders are that lucky. Fortunately, there is the Internet, specifically YouTube. A quick YouTube search for "Shakespeare" can unearth thousands of results, many appropriate for the classroom.

The first "Hamlet" result showed an 18-year-old African-American actor on the streets of Camden, New Jersey, delivering a riveting performance of Hamlet's "The play's the thing." The second clip was from *Cat Head Theatre,* an animation of cats performing Hamlet. Of course, YouTube boasts not just alley cats and feline thespians, but also clips by true legends of the stage, such as John Gielgud and Richard Burton. These clips can be saved and shown in classrooms, providing useful inspiration.

One advantage of the amazing variety of clips available on YouTube is that students can witness the wide range of interpretations for any given scene, speech, or character in Shakespeare, thus freeing them from any preconceived notion that there is a "right" way to do it. Furthermore, modern interpretations of the Bard may appeal to those who are put off by the "thees and thous" of Elizabethan speech.

By seeing Shakespeare performed either live or on film, students are able to hear the cadence, rhythm, vocal dynamics, and pronunciation of the language, and they can appreciate the life that other actors breathe into the characters. They get to see the story told dramatically, which inspires them to tell their own version.

PUTTING IT ALL TOGETHER

THE STEPS

After a few sessions of theater games to warm up the group, it's time to begin the process of casting the play. Each play cutting in *The 30-Minute Shakespeare* series includes a cast list and a sample program, demonstrating which parts have been divided. Cast size is generally between twelve and thirty students, with major roles frequently assigned to more than one performer. In other words, one student may play Juliet in the first scene, another in the second scene, and yet another in the third. This will distribute the parts evenly so that there is no "star of the show." Furthermore, this prevents actors from being burdened with too many lines. If I have an actor who is particularly talented or enthusiastic, I will give her a bigger role. It is important to go with the grain—one cast member's enthusiasm can be contagious.

I provide the performer of each shared role with a similar headpiece and/or cape, so that the audience can keep track of the characters. When there are sets of twins, I try to use blue shirts and red shirts, so that the audience has at least a fighting chance of figuring it out! Other than these costume consistencies, I rely on the text and the audience's observance to sort out the doubling of characters. Generally, the audience can follow because we are telling the story.

Some participants are shy and do not wish to speak at all on stage. To these students I assign non-speaking parts and technical roles such as sound operator and stage manager. However, I always get everybody on stage at some point, even if it is just for the final group speech, because I want every group member to experience what it is like to be on a stage as part of an ensemble.

CASTING THE PLAY

Young people can be self-conscious and nervous with "formal" auditions, especially if they have little or no acting experience.

I conduct what I call an "informal" audition process. I hand out a questionnaire asking students if there is any particular role that they desire, whether they play a musical instrument. To get a feel for them as people, I also ask them to list one or two hobbies or interests. Occasionally this will inform my casting decisions. If someone can juggle, and the play has the part of a Fool, that skill may come in handy. Dancing or martial arts abilities can also be applied to roles.

For the auditions, I do not use the cut script. I have students stand and read from the Folger edition of the complete text in order to hear how they fare with the longer passages. I encourage them to breathe and carry their vocal energy all the way to the end of a long line of text. I also urge them to play with diction, projection, modulation, and dynamics, elements of speech that we have worked on in our vocal warm-ups and theater games.

I base my casting choices largely on reading ability, vocal strength, and enthusiasm for the project. If someone has requested a particular role, I try to honor that request. I explain that even with a small part, an actor can create a vivid character that adds a lot to the play. Wide variations in personality types can be utilized: if there are two students cast as Romeo, one brooding and one effusive, I try to put the more brooding Romeo in an early lovelorn scene, and place the effusive Romeo in the balcony scene. Occasionally one gets lucky, and the doubling of characters provides a way to match personality types with different aspects of a character's personality. But also be aware of the potential serendipity of non-traditional casting. For example, I have had one of the smallest students in the class play a powerful Othello. True power comes from within!

Generally, I have more females than males in a class, so women are more likely (and more willing) to play male characters than vice versa.

Rare is the high school boy who is brave enough to play a female character, which is unfortunate because it can reap hilarious results.

GET OUTSIDE HELP

Every time there is a fight scene in one of the plays I am directing, I call on my friend Michael Tolaydo, a professional actor and theater professor at St. Mary's College, who is an expert in all aspects of theater, including fight choreography. Not only does Michael stage the fight, but he does so in a way that furthers the action of the play, highlighting character's traits and bringing out the best in the student actors. Fight choreography must be done by an expert or somebody could get hurt. In the absence of such help, super slow-motion fights are always a safe bet and can be quite effective, especially when accompanied by a soundtrack on the boom box.

During dress rehearsals I invite my friend Hilary Kacser. a Washington-area actor and dialect coach for two decades. Because I bring her in late in the rehearsal process, I have her direct her comments to me, which I then filter and relay to the cast. This avoids confusing the cast with a second set of directions. This caveat only applies to general directorial comments from outside visitors. Comments on specific artistic disciplines such as dance, music, and stage combat can come from the outside experts themselves.

If you work in a school, you might have helpful resources within your own building, such as a music or dance teacher who could contribute their expertise to a scene. If nobody is available in your school, try seeking out a member of the local professional theater. Many local performing artists will be glad to help, and the students are usually thrilled to have a visit from a professional performer.

LET STUDENTS BRING THEMSELVES INTO THE PLAY

The best ideas often come from the students themselves. If a young actor has a notion of how to play a scene, I will always give that idea a try. In a rehearsal of *Henry IV, Part 1,* one traveler jumped into the other's arms when they were robbed. It got a huge laugh. This was something that they did on instinct. We kept that bit for the performance, and it worked wonderfully.

As a director, you have to foster an environment in which that kind of spontaneity can occur. The students have to feel safe to experiment. In the same production of *Henry IV*, Falstaff and Hal invented a little fist bump "secret handshake" to use in the battle scene. The students were having fun and bringing parts of themselves into the play. Shakespeare himself would have approved. When possible I try to err on the side of fun because if the young actors are having fun, then they will commit themselves to the project. The beauty of the language, the story, the characters, and the pathos will follow.

There is a balance to be achieved here, however. In that same production of *Henry IV, Part 1,* the student who played Bardolph was having a great time with her character. She carried a leather wineskin around and offered it up to the other characters in the tavern. It was a prop with which she developed a comic relationship. At the end of our thirty-minute *Henry IV, Part 1,* I added a scene from *Henry IV, Part 2* as a coda: The new King Henry V (formerly Falstaff's drinking and carousing buddy Hal) rejects Falstaff, banishing him from within ten miles of the King. It is a sad and sobering moment, one of the most powerful in the play.

But at the performance, in the middle of the King's rejection speech (played by a female student, and her only speech), Bardolph offered her flask to King Henry and got a big laugh, thus not only upstaging the King but also undermining the seriousness and poignancy of the whole scene. She did not know any better; she was bringing herself to the character as I had been encouraging her to do. But it was inappropriate, and in subsequent seasons, if I foresaw something like that happening as an individual joyfully occupied a character, I attempted to prevent it. Some things we cannot predict. Now I make sure to issue a statement warning against changing any of the blocking on show day, and to watch out for upstaging one's peers.

FOUR FORMS OF ENGAGEMENT: VOCAL, EMOTIONAL, PHYSICAL, AND INTELLECTUAL

When directing a Shakespeare play with a group of students, I always start with the words themselves because the words have the power to engage the emotions, mind, and body. Also, I start with the words in action, as in the previously mentioned exercise, "Positive and Negative Salutations." Students become physically engaged; their bodies react to the images the words evoke. The words have the power to trigger a switch in both the teller and the listener, eliciting both an emotional and physical reaction. I have never heard a student utter the line "Fie! Fie! You counterfeit, you puppet you!" without seeing him change before my eyes. His spine stiffens, his eyes widen, and his fingers point menacingly.

Having used Shakespeare's words to engage the students emotionally and physically, one can then return to the text for a more reflective discussion of what the words mean to us personally. I always make sure to leave at least a few class periods open for discussion of the text, line by line, to ensure that students understand intellectually what they feel viscerally. The advantage to a performance-based teaching of Shakespeare is that by engaging students vocally, emotionally, and physically, it is then much easier to engage them intellectually because they are invested in the words, the characters, and the story. We always start on our feet, and later we sit and talk.

SIX ELEMENTS OF DRAMA: PLOT, CHARACTER, THEME, DICTION, MUSIC, AND SPECTACLE

Over two thousand years ago, Aristotle's *Poetics* outlined six elements of drama, in order of importance: Plot, Character, Theme, Diction, Music, and Spectacle. Because Shakespeare was foremost a playwright, it is helpful to take a brief look at these six elements as they relate to directing a Shakespeare play in the classroom.

PLOT (ACTION)

To Aristotle, plot was the most important element. One of the purposes of *The 30-Minute Shakespeare* is to provide a script that tells Shakespeare's stories, as opposed to concentrating on one scene. In a thirty-minute edit of a Shakespeare play, some plot elements are necessarily omitted. For the sake of a full understanding of the characters' relationships and motivations, it is helpful to make short plot summaries of each scene so that students are aware of their characters' arcs throughout the play. The scene descriptions in the Folger editions are sufficient to fill in the plot holes. Students can read the descriptions aloud during class time to ensure that the story is clear and that no plot elements are neglected. Additionally, there are one-page charts in the Folger editions of *Shakespeare Set Free*, indicating characters' relations graphically, with lines connecting families and factions to give students a visual representation of what can often be complex interrelationships, particularly in Shakespeare's history plays.

Young actors love action. That is why *The 30-Minute Shakespeare* includes dynamic blocking (stage direction) that allows students to tell the story in a physically dramatic fashion. Characters' movements on the stage are always motivated by the text itself.

CHARACTER

I consider myself a facilitator and a director more than an acting teacher. I want the students' understanding of their characters to spring from the text and the story. From there, I encourage them to consider how their character might talk, walk, stand, sit, eat, and drink. I also urge students to consider characters' motivations, objectives, and relationships, and I will ask pointed questions to that end during the rehearsal process. I try not to show the students how I would perform a scene, but if no ideas are forthcoming from anybody in the class, I will suggest a minimum of two possibilities for how the character might respond.

At times students may want more guidance and examples. Over thirteen years of directing plays in the classroom, I have wavered between wanting all the ideas to come from the students, and deciding that I need to be more of a "director," telling them what I would like to see them doing. It is a fine line, but in recent years I have decided that if I don't see enough dynamic action or characterization, I will step in and "direct" more. But I always make sure to leave room for students to bring themselves into the characters because their own ideas are invariably the best.

THEME (THOUGHTS, IDEAS)

In a typical English classroom, theme will be a big topic for discussion of a Shakespeare play. Using a performance-based method of teaching Shakespeare, an understanding of the play's themes develops from "mining the text" and exploring Shakespeare's words and his story. If the students understand what they are saying and how that relates to their characters and the overall story, the plays' themes will emerge clearly. We always return to the text itself. There are a number of elegant computer programs, such as www.wordle.net, that will count the number of recurring words in a passage and illustrate them graphically. For example, if the word "jealousy" comes up more than any other word in *Othello,* it will appear in a larger font. Seeing the words displayed by size in this way can offer up illuminating insights into the interaction between words in the text and the play's themes. Your computer-minded students might enjoy searching for such tidbits. There are more internet tools and websites in the Additional Resources section at the back of this book.

I cannot overstress the importance of acting out the play in understanding its themes. By embodying the roles of Othello and Iago and reciting their words, students do not simply comprehend the themes intellectually, but understand them kinesthetically, physically, and emotionally. They are essentially *living* the characters' jealousy, pride, and feelings about race. The themes of appearance vs.

reality, good vs. evil, honesty, misrepresentation, and self-knowledge (or lack thereof) become physically felt as well as intellectually understood. Performing Shakespeare delivers a richer understanding than that which comes from just reading the play. Students can now relate the characters' conflicts to their own struggles.

DICTION (LANGUAGE)

If I had to cite one thing I would like my actors to take from their experience of performing a play by William Shakespeare, it is an appreciation and understanding of the beauty of Shakespeare's language. The language is where it all begins and ends. Shakespeare's stories are dramatic, his characters are rich and complex, and his settings are exotic and fascinating, but it is through his language that these all achieve their richness. This leads me to spend more time on language than on any other element of the performance.

Starting with daily vocal warm-ups, many of them using parts of the script or other Shakespearean passages, I consistently emphasize the importance of the words. Young actors often lack experience in speaking clearly and projecting their voices outward, so in addition to comprehension, I emphasize projection, diction, breathing, pacing, dynamics, coloring of words, and vocal energy. *Theatre Games for Young Performers* contains many effective vocal exercises, as does the Folger's *Shakespeare Set Free* series. Consistent emphasis on all aspects of Shakespeare's language, especially on how to speak it effectively, is the most important element to any Shakespeare performance with a young cast.

MUSIC

A little music can go a long way in setting a mood for a thirty-minute Shakespeare play. I usually open the show with a short passage of music to set the tone. Thirty seconds of music played on a boom box operated by a student can provide a nice introduction to the play, create an atmosphere for the audience, and give the actors a sense of place and feeling.

iTunes is a good starting point for choosing your music. Typing in "Shakespeare" or "Hamlet" or "jealousy" (if you are going for a theme) will result in an excellent selection of aural performance enhancers at the very reasonable price of ninety-nine cents each (or free of charge, see Additional Resources section). Likewise, fight sounds, foreboding sounds, weather sounds (rain, thunder), trumpet sounds, etc. are all readily available online at affordable cost. I typically include three sound cues in a play, just enough to enhance but not overpower a production. The boom box operator sits on the far right or left of the stage, not backstage, so he can see the action. This also has the added benefit of having somebody out there with a script, capable of prompting in a pinch.

SPECTACLE

Aristotle considered spectacle the least important aspect of drama. Students tend to be surprised at this since we are used to being bombarded with production values on TV and video, often at the expense of substance. In my early days of putting on student productions, I would find myself hamstrung by my own ambitions in the realm of scenic design.

A simple bench or two chairs set on the stage are sufficient. The sense of "place" can be achieved through language and acting. Simple set dressing, a few key props, and some tasteful, emblematic costume pieces will go a long way toward providing all the "spectacle" you need.

In the stage directions to the plays in *The 30-Minute Shakespeare* series, I make frequent use of two large pillars stage left and right at the Folger Shakespeare Library's Elizabethan Theatre. I also have characters frequently entering and exiting from "stage rear." Your stage will have a different layout. Take a good look at the performing space you will be using and see if there are any elements that can be incorporated into your own stage directions. Is there a balcony? Can characters enter from the audience? (Make sure that they can get there from backstage, unless you want them waiting in the lobby until their entrance, which may be impractical.) If possible, make sure to rehearse in that space a few times to fix any technical issues and perhaps discover a few fun staging variations that will add pizzazz and dynamics to your own show.

The real spectacle is in the telling of the tale. Wooden swords are handy for characters that need them. Students should be warned at the outset that playing with swords outside of the scene is verboten. Letters, moneybags, and handkerchiefs should all have plentiful duplicates kept in a small prop box, as well as with a stage manager, because they tend to disappear in the hands of adolescents. After every rehearsal and performance, I recommend you personally sweep the rehearsal or performance area immediately for stray props. It is amazing what gets left behind.

Ultimately, the performances are about language and human drama, not set pieces, props, and special effects. Fake blood, glitter, glass, and liquids have no place on the stage; they are a recipe for disaster, or, at the very least, a big mess. On the other hand, the props that are employed can often be used effectively to convey character, as in Bardolph's aforementioned relationship with his wineskin.

PITFALLS AND SOLUTIONS

Putting on a play in a high school classroom is not easy. There are problems with enthusiasm, attitude, attention, and line memorization, to name a few. As anybody who has directed a play will tell you, it is always darkest before the dawn. My experience is that after one or two days of utter despair just before the play goes up, show day breaks and the play miraculously shines. To quote a recurring gag in one of my favorite movies, *Shakespeare in Love:* "It's a mystery."

ENTHUSIASM, FRUSTRATION, AND DISCIPLINE

Bring the enthusiasm yourself. Feed on the energy of the eager students, and others will pick up on that. Keep focused on the task at hand. Arrive prepared. Enthusiasm comes as you make headway. Ultimately, it helps to remind the students that a play is fun. I try to focus on the positive attributes of the students, rather than the ones that drive me crazy. This is easier said than done, but it is important. One season, I yelled at the group two days in a row. On day two of yelling, they tuned me out, and it took me a while to win them back. I learned my lesson; since then I've tried not to raise my voice out of anger or frustration. As I grow older and more mature, it is important for me to lead by example. It has been years since I yelled at a student group. If I am disappointed in their work or their behavior, I will express my disenchantment in words, speaking from the heart as somebody who cares about them and cares about our performance and our experience together. I find that fundamentally, young people want to please, to do well, and to be liked. If there is a serious discipline problem, I will hand it over to the regular classroom teacher, the administrator, or the parent.

LINE MEMORIZATION

Students may have a hard time memorizing lines. In these cases, see if you can pair them up with a "buddy" and existing friend who will run lines with them in person or over the phone after school. If students do not have such a "buddy," I volunteer to run lines with them myself. If serious line memorization problems arise that cannot be solved through work, then two students can switch parts if it is early enough in the rehearsal process. For doubled roles, the scene with fewer lines can go to the actor who is having memorization problems. Additionally, a few passages or lines can be cut. Again, it is important to address these issues early. Later cuts become more problematic as other actors have already memorized their cues. I have had to do late cuts about twice in thirteen years. While they have gotten us out of jams, it is best to assess early whether a student will have line memorization problems, and deal with the problem sooner rather than later.

In production, always keep several copies of the script backstage, as well as cheat sheets indicating cues, entrances, and scene changes. Make a prop list, indicating props for each scene, as well as props that are the responsibility of individual actors. Direct the Stage Manager and an Assistant Stage Manager to keep track of these items, and on show days, personally double-check if you can.

In thirteen years of preparing an inner-city public high school English class for a public performance on a field trip to the Folger Secondary School Shakespeare Festival, my groups and I have been beset by illness, emotional turmoil, discipline problems, stage fright, adolescent angst, midlife crises (not theirs), and all manner of other emergencies, including acts of God and nature. Despite the difficulties and challenges inherent in putting on a Shakespeare play with a group of young people, one amazing fact stands out in my experience. Here is how many times a student has been absent for show day: Zero. Somehow, everybody has always made it to the show, and the show has gone on. How can this be? It's a mystery.

✳ PERFORMANCE NOTES: *THE TEMPEST*

I directed this version of *The Tempest* in 2011 with a group of high school seniors. The play is ideal for young actors and allows them to enter a fantastic new world full of colorful characters and beguiling language. These notes are the result of my own review of the performance video. They are not intended to be the "definitive" performance notes for all productions of *The Tempest*. Your production will be unique to you and your cast. That is the magic of live theater.

What is interesting about these notes is that many of the performance details I mention were not part of the original stage directions. They either emerged spontaneously on performance day or were developed by students in rehearsal after the stage directions had been written into the script. Some of these pieces of stage business will work like a charm. Others may fall flat. Still others might be unintentionally hilarious.

My favorites are the ones that arise directly from the students themselves and demonstrate a union between actor and character, as if that individual has become a vehicle for the character she is playing. To witness an eighteen-year-old young woman "become" Prospero as Shakespeare's words leave her mouth is a memorable moment indeed.

SCENE 1 (ACT I, SCENE I)

The play begins on a ship at sea in the midst of a storm. To set the mood and place, pre-recorded storm sounds play throughout the scene. Prospero stands upstage with his staff, directing the tempest. In this way, the audience perceives his magical powers from the outset. The volume of the storm sounds must be loud enough to require the actors to raise their voices to be heard. A live drum played offstage will simulate thunder and provide the cue for all shipmates to lurch simultaneously toward stage right and then back to stage center.

As the Boatswain yells at Antonio and Gonzalo downstage center, the ship's crew pantomimes pulling a rope tight upstage. The effect is one of frenetic activity verging on panic. The drums beat thunder once again and now all shipmates lurch to stage right and then back to center. At the end of the scene, Gonzalo hangs onto a pillar as if it were a mast and recites his final line, "Now would I give a thousand furlongs of sea for an acre of barren ground." By the conclusion of a very short scene, we have established characters and place and determined that danger and magic are afoot.

SCENE 2 (ACT I, SCENE II)

Simple sound effects played live contribute to the air of magic in this scene. When Prospero waves his hand to put Miranda to sleep, the sound operator strikes a "ding" on the triangle, and as Ariel enters for the first time, she plays the recorder. For my 2011 production, I gave a basic recorder instruction to the actresses cast in the role. Likewise with drums and triangle, I imparted my musical knowledge to the cast, many of whom had never played these instruments. If you as director do not have musical ability or experience yourself, bring in an outside expert to impart a brief lesson in the instruments used in the play. If necessary, enlist the expertise of other colleagues for help with other performance skills such as dance choreography and stage combat.

The actress who played Ariel in this scene skipped and spun around while she walked, her eyes twinkling with the magic of her character. In later scenes, another student portrayed Ariel. When you have two actors splitting a role, encourage them to watch each other play the part and, if possible, find a common theatrical vocabulary:

physical mannerisms or vocal inflections that identify the character. This will make it easier for the audience to understand the transition, and reinforce to the actors that a person's uniqueness can be depicted using specific techniques. (For example, consider how a character stands or walks and then try to illustrate that physically.) Emphasize that the text is the first and best place to look for clues about a role. Encourage your actors to investigate not only what their characters say, but also what other characters say about them.

Ariel uses scarves to accent her movements, holding one in each hand and swinging them about herself gracefully. Often the simplest of props and costume pieces add much to a character's look and overall dramatic impression. Prospero has a staff that he uses both to lean on, contributing to his appearance as an old man, and as a magic wand. Perhaps his years fall away when he uses his magic, allowing him to wave the staff with a youthful vigor, but when he is back to his more mortal self, the years return and he is older again. Actors should be instructed that props are tools by which an actor reveals elements of his character. How we interact with the physical world speaks volumes about who we are.

Every prop, set piece, and costume piece gives actors an opportunity to reveal to the audience more about themselves. Ariel, Prospero, Caliban, Miranda, and the Boatswain will all sit on a stool in a different way. For an interesting rehearsal exercise, place a stool on the stage and have your players enter and sit down one by one, using the gait and physical demeanor of their characters. By discussing the differences in each character's "sitting style," you can yield interesting insights into his or her unique personality.

SCENE 3 (ACT II, SCENE II)

In our production, the Narrator gave a small wink at the end of her line, "Drunk Stephano finds them both and shares his bottle . . . which livens things up." This garnered a nice laugh from the audience. I am continually reminded how small details in delivery make a large difference in the overall effect of a line and, subsequently, the tenor of the production. We humans each have a distinct spark in us, and when an actor chooses to share that light by adding a bit of spirit to a piece of text, magic happens. I try to impress this upon the actors. Each individual contributes something special to the production that only she possesses. A great piece of art is not just technique and talent—it is spirit as well.

This is a spirited scene, and the actress playing Caliban embodied that exuberance. She gamely donned a furry monster's outfit, complete with big hairy costume feet and ridiculous horns, and threw herself into the role, beginning by diving flat onto the stage to hide under her blanket upon seeing Trinculo. Costuming can help an actor get into character. Playing with hats early in the rehearsal process loosens up young actors and helps develop their sense of "play." If a character requires ungainly costuming, such as with Caliban's big feet, make sure to introduce that costume piece early enough into the rehearsal process for the actor to become accustomed to it and incorporate it into her character's personality.

Visibility is also important in this scene. Trinculo and Caliban lie head to foot, perpendicular to the audience, with two feet sticking out either end of the blanket. Caliban should be downstage of Trinculo so the audience can see his wide-eyed expression as he drinks and speaks. Trinculo can rise to a sitting position on key lines and then fall back down; Caliban can do the same so that the two heads are performing a kind of seesaw dance with each other.

The three students playing Caliban, Trinculo, and Stephano exploited the comic potential of this classic trio. Trinculo's hysterical commentary on Caliban's fishy qualities calls for a childlike curiosity that this actress possessed, and Stephano's endearing drunken leadership anchored the scene in cheerful chaos. At the end of the scene, the three characters paraded about the stage in a circle, raising their arms and shouting, "Hie-day, freedom!" Their exit, a choreographed boogie dance incorporating hand gestures, foot stomping, and hip shaking, received wild approval from the audience.

This scene should be played broadly and joyously, with emphasis on the raw emotions conjured by the text: fear (of both the elements and strange beings) and joy (at the reunion of friends, the discovery of "celestial" liquor, and the new freedoms discovered on this magical island). There are some dark turns ahead in this Shakespearean fantasy, but in this scene, the world is full of merriment, hope, and silliness.

SCENE 4 (ACT III, SCENE I)

Small pieces of stage business are often quite effective at setting the tone. This scene, for example, has an innocent sweetness to it. To convey this, Ferdinand drops his pile of logs upon spying Miranda, as if her beauty has usurped control of his body. He then earnestly and chivalrously prevents Miranda from picking up the logs and gently leads her back to her seat, where he woos her on his knees. Throughout the scene, Prospero stands at rear, observing the pair's exchange. He is amused and delighted that his plan to unite the two is taking shape, and his background reactions (smiling, chuckling, etc.) can reflect that joy.

In our 2011 production, two naturally shy students played the roles of Ferdinand and Miranda, which added to the comic awkwardness of the characters' interchanges. Despite her shyness, the actress playing Miranda had a clear grasp of the "game playing" nature of her character's lines to Ferdinand, and her innocence was undercut by a clear sense that she was in control.

Actors can experiment with status by first playing the scene with Miranda as "high status" and then doing the same with Ferdinand, taking note of what the difference yields. Either character can be played as "low status" as well, yielding four possible sets of results. For example, if Miranda is playing her part as "high status," she will easily lead Ferdinand back to the stool when saying, "Work not so hard: rest yourself." If Ferdinand is also playing "high status," however, then he will resist being led back to the stool and instead gallantly lead Miranda. Any moment in the text can be reinterpreted using simple theater techniques, which often yield fascinating revelations on how to play the interactions and the scenes themselves.

As with many of Shakespeare's phrases, Prospero's final line in this scene is tricky to understand at first reading: "So glad of this as they I cannot be, / Who are surprised withal; but my rejoicing / At nothing can be more." (Roughly translated, he is stating, "I cannot be as happy as these surprised kids, but nothing could make me happier.) The syntax and placement of words is unusual. Make sure your actors know exactly what they are saying and what this means both to their characters and to themselves personally. Work out the meaning of the lines together as a group for maximum participation and interpretive possibilities. If alternative meanings other than my own emerge from this dissection of the lines, we are all the richer for it.

SCENE 5 (ACT III, SCENE II)

I am always excited when actors inject spark into tiny parts or seemingly minor lines. In the introduction to this scene, the Narrator explains that Caliban has urged Stephano to kill Prospero, exclaiming, "What a monstrous thing to do!" As the Narrator in our production recited this line, she held up her hands like claws and growled the word "monstrous" in a delightfully guttural roar. She then finished with a shiver, as if terrified herself at this prospect. As this actress adeptly demonstrated, there are no small roles.

Caliban takes a swig from Stephano's cup, but it is a bit larger gulp than expected. The monster drains the cup dry and holds it upside down over her mouth as if waiting for more liquor to magically fall. This small piece of stage business can go far in revealing Caliban's animal attraction to alcohol.

As the play progresses, the trio of Caliban, Trinculo and Stephano becomes increasingly inebriated, which opens the door to some broader comedy. Caliban and Trinculo's argument—spurred by the invisible Ariel's deceptive asides—can be louder and more physically demonstrative than their previous physicalizations, due to the liquor's effects.

After hearing Ariel's initial "thou liest," Caliban and Trinculo square off as if to fight. Following her second "thou liest," Stephano hits Trinculo with his hat. This sends Trinculo into a pout, which is soon cured by Stephano's invitation for him to join Caliban as one of his "viceroys." The emotions should change quickly due to the characters' intoxication. Have your actors experiment with different ways of playing a drunkard. Encourage them to explore the emotional dynamics that come with overindulging rather than relying solely on physical moves such as stumbling. Trinculo, for example, may become more jealous of Caliban as he consumes more alcohol.

By the end of the scene, the trio's emotions have settled on happiness. As in their last scene together, the characters dance offstage, singing merrily. Just as tragedy gives audience and actor a chance to purge themselves of pity and fear, so a comedy allows us to find emotional release through the laughter that Shakespeare's words and characters joyfully provoke.

SCENE 6 (ACT III, SCENE III)

This scene provides a great opportunity for actors to stretch out into the fantasy world of the play. During the Strange Shapes sequence, players dance in a freeform style to otherworldly music. (To draw the most inspired responses from your actors, choose music that is truly strange and arresting.) Improvised dancing is not the only choice, as the Strange Shapes could perform a choreographed set of movements instead.

As with any production, the staging for this play is wholly dependent on the director's individual vision coupled with the group's skills and preferences. Even if you choose to stage your version exactly as outlined here, your production will come with its own unique and inimitable elements. That is the magic of live theater: no two productions are alike. Scene Six, in particular, allows for plenty of freedom to experiment with sound and movement and to revel in pure imaginative play.

The role of Ariel as Harpy affords this actor a chance to stretch as well. Performers always have fun playing animals and non-human characters, and *The Tempest* offers several: Caliban, three dogs, and the large, winged Harpy. In our production, the actress playing Ariel as Harpy had a great time inserting her own "Braack!" in between lines, coupled with a hunched ruffling of her "wings." She wore a simple costume bird mask and became, as young actors often do, even more alive under the mask's anonymity. When the Harpy finished her dire proclamation to the astonished island visitors, she returned upstage to observe the rest of the scene with Prospero, responding not as the masked, harsh, and frightening Harpy, but as the unmasked, gentle, and delighted Ariel. This change in demeanor between a masked and unmasked player gave her an opportunity to demonstrate the power of the mask in eliciting quick and distinct character changes.

Explore with your actors the possibilities inherent in playing animal images with their human characters, too. If Prospero were an animal, which one would he be? How about Stephano?

The Strange Shapes can also experiment with animal images, since it is unclear in the text what they really are. Try experimenting with the Strange Shapes as a herd of antelopes, flock of birds, pride of lions, or group of other contrasting animals such as chimpanzees or elephants. There is great variety and personality in the animal kingdom that actors can use to inform their movements, especially in a fantasy where strange beasts are already part of the story.

SCENE 7 (ACT IV, SCENE I)

The appearance of the three dogs in this scene adds another non-human note of hilarity. During rehearsals for our production, we explored how Caliban, Stephano, and Trinculo would react to being chased by a dog: Stephano, being a drunk, would offer the dog some alcohol from his flask, whereas Caliban would square off with the dog as if to fight, ultimately scaring the whimpering and whining animal away. Players can refine each scene by mining the text, i.e., studying the words carefully for their literal and poetic meaning. By doing so, actors will develop a rounded and rich understanding of their characters.

Animal costumes, similar to musical recordings and set dressings, provide opportunities for cast members to add their artistic inspiration and contribute to the production as a whole. Likewise, programs, costumes, and outside research (dramaturgy) all add to the play, and thus non-actors can significantly enrich our dramatic work. I favor stripped-down productions with a greater emphasis on storytelling over stage effects. Nonetheless, a handmade set of dog ears will certainly add pizzazz to any Shakespearean comedy and inspire the actors wearing them to new heights of hilarity.

SCENE 8 (ACT V, SCENE I)

The Narrator for this scene once again seized an opportunity for a laugh by pausing between the words "This must be" and "a Shakespearean comedy" to offer her own whimsical hand gesture. Her eyes lit up and she smiled brightly, bringing the audience into her joy. We cannot teach actors how to connect with the audience, but we can encourage them to approach the play with originality and merriment.

Prospero forgot his next line during one performance of this scene, resulting in a long pause. Always have a prompter ready offstage, as this can prevent a production from grinding to a halt due to line memorization problems or nerves. With a brief prompt, the scene regains its momentum and the day is saved! As director, I sit in the audience with a script, and on a few occasions, I have prompted actors from my seat when it was clear that no other solution was forthcoming.

As with many of the Bard's plays, the conclusion of *The Tempest* becomes a bit crowded with actors. The simplest solution is often the best: have the performers form a semicircle across the stage to ensure greatest visibility. If one character is at odds with the group, she can stand off to one side to indicate the schism. Here, Caliban can separate himself from Stephano, realizing that he has been worshiping a "dull fool." During the final scene of a Shakespearean comedy, couples should unite so the audience can see their relationships come together. In this case, Miranda and Ferdinand join hands as Alonso stands on Ferdinand's other side, hand on his shoulder.

This bittersweet and fantastical comedy comes to a close with the entire group reciting the line, "We are such stuff as dreams are made of, and our little life is rounded with a sleep." (In our production, the three panting dogs lay down loyally in front of the humans.) Actors should inject a rising vocal energy into this final speech as they raise their arms in unison, follow the cue of Prospero, and bow happily, the proud young owners of a classic and enduring Shakespearean comedy.

Live theater is magical. It is the most dynamic form of entertainment available to us. There is nothing like the interchange between actors and audience, that vibrant energy that is created in the theatre. *The Tempest* is one of Shakespeare's most poetic, magical, and moving tales, and we are fortunate to be able to continue giving it life, especially with young performers who can give it the vitality it deserves.

✳ *THE TEMPEST:* SET AND PROP LIST

SET PIECES:

> Two stools
> Chair
> Banquet table

PROPS:

THROUGHOUT:

> Staff for Prospero
> Recorder for Ariel

SCENE 1:

> Rope for sailors

SCENE 2:

> Cape or cloak for Prospero

SCENE 3:

> Bundle of wood for Caliban
> Cloak for Caliban
> Flask for Stephano

SCENE 4:

> Bundle of wood for Ferdinand

SCENE 5:

Glasses or flasks for Caliban, Stephano, and Trinculo

Hat for Stephano

SCENE 6:

Swords for Alonso, Sebastian, and Antonio

Mask for Ariel

SCENE 8:

Cape or cloak for Prospero

Benjamin Banneker Academic High School presents

The Tempest
By William Shakespeare
Folger Secondary School Shakespeare Festival

Tuesday, March 22nd, 2011
Senior English Class | Instructor: Mr. Leo Bowman
Guest Director: Mr. Nick Newlin

CAST:

Scene 1: On a ship at sea
Narrator: Bria Petty
Master: Byan Frazier
Boatswain: Brandon Conway
Alonso (King of Naples): Gerald Allen
Antonio (Duke of Milan): Mia Hall
Gonzalo (Counselor to Alonzo): Chrisa Williams
Sebastian (Alonso's brother): Josué Garcia
Sailors: Andrea Isaac, Sabrina Candelario, Sayon Doré

Scene 2: On the island
Narrator: Fidelia Igwe
Prospero (Former Duke of Milan): Bria Petty
Miranda (his daughter): Shelby Adkins
Ariel (a spirit, servant to Prospero): Daisha Hale
Ferdinand (King Alonso's son): Kendl Gordy

Scene 3: Another part of the island
Narrator: Mia Hall
Caliban (inhabitant of the island): Deja Harrison
Trinculo (servant to Alonso): Franiqua Williams
Stephano (Alonso's butler): Shameka Jones

Scene 4: Before Prospero's cell
Narrator: Monique Brevard
Ferdinand: Javier Claros
Miranda: Tranesha Hines
Prospero: Briana Clorey

Scene 5: Another part of the island
Narrator: Chrisa Williams
Stephano: Andrea Isaac
Caliban: Deja Harrison
Trinculo: Franiqua Williams
Ariel: Fidelia Igwe

Scene 6: Another part of the island
Narrator: Kelly Williams
Gonzalo: Chrisa Williams
Alonso: Adrienne Fenton
Antonio: Kristie Wheeler
Sebastian: Josué Garcia
Ariel: Fidelia Igwe
Prospero: Aarrayn Perez
Strange Shapes: Franiqua Williams, Sabrina Candelario, Bria Petty

Scene 7: Before Prospero's cell
Narrator: Andrea Isaac
Ferdinand: Javier Claros
Prospero: Laura Washington
Ariel: Sabrina Candelario
Miranda: Emoni Smith
Stephano: Gerald Allen

Trinculo: Franiqua Williams
Caliban: Deja Harrison
Dogs: Mia Hall, Josué Garcia,
Kendl Gordy

Scene 8: Before Prospero's cell
Narrator: Laura Washington
Ariel: Sabrina Candelario
Gonzalo: Chrisa Williams
Alonso: Adrienne Fenton
Sebastian: Bryan Frazier
Antonio: Kristie Wheeler
Ferdinand: Javier Claros
Miranda: Emoni Smith
Trinculo: Franiqua Williams
Stephano: Gerald Allen
Caliban: Deja Harrison
Boatswain: Brandon Conway

Stage Manager: Kelly Williams
Assistant Stage Manager: Sayon Doré
Boombox and sound effects: Tiara Davis
Props and stage crew: Heidy Marquez
Costumes and stage crew: Claudia Martinez

ADDITIONAL RESOURCES

SHAKESPEARE

Shakespeare Set Free: Teaching Romeo and Juliet, Macbeth and a Midsummer Night's Dream
Peggy O'Brien, Ed., Teaching Shakespeare Institute
Washington Square Press
New York, 1993

Shakespeare Set Free: Teaching Hamlet and Henry IV, Part 1
Peggy O'Brien, Ed., Teaching Shakespeare Institute
Washington Square Press
New York, 1994

Shakespeare Set Free: Teaching Twelfth Night and Othello
Peggy O'Brien, Ed., Teaching Shakespeare Institute
Washington Square Press
New York, 1995

The *Shakespeare Set Free* series is an invaluable resource with lesson plans, activites, handouts, and excellent suggestions for rehearsing and performing Shakespeare plays in a classroom setting.

ShakesFear and How to Cure It!
Ralph Alan Cohen
Prestwick House, Inc.
Delaware, 2006

The Friendly Shakespeare: A Thoroughly Painless Guide to the Best of the Bard
Norrie Epstein
Penguin Books
New York, 1994

Brush Up Your Shakespeare!
Michael Macrone
Cader Books
New York, 1990

Shakespeare's Insults: Educating Your Wit
Wayne F. Hill and Cynthia J. Ottchen
Three Rivers Press
New York, 1991

Practical Approaches to Teaching Shakespeare
Peter Reynolds
Oxford University Press
New York, 1991

Scenes From Shakespeare:
A Workbook for Actors
Robin J. Holt
McFarland and Co.
London, 1988

THEATER AND PERFORMANCE

Impro: Improvisation and the Theatre
Keith Johnstone
Routledge Books
London, 1982

A Dictionary of Theatre Anthropology:
The Secret Art of the Performer
Eugenio Barba and Nicola Savarese
Routledge
London, 1991

THEATER GAMES

Theatre Games for Young Performers
Maria C. Novelly
Meriwether Publishing
Colorado, 1990

Improvisation for the Theater
Viola Spolin
Northwestern University Press
Illinois, 1983

Theater Games for Rehearsal:
A Director's Handbook
Viola Spolin
Northwestern University Press
Illinois, 1985

101 Theatre Games for Drama
Teachers, Classroom Teachers
& Directors
Mila Johansen
Players Press Inc.
California, 1994

PLAY DIRECTING

Theater and the Adolescent Actor:
Building a Successful School Program
Camille L. Poisson
Archon Books
Connecticut, 1994

Directing for the Theatre
W. David Sievers
Wm. C. Brown, Co.
Iowa, 1965

The Director's Vision: Play Direction
from Analysis to Production
Louis E. Catron
Mayfield Publishing Co.
California, 1989

INTERNET RESOURCES

http://www.folger.edu
The Folger Shakespeare Library's
website has lesson plans, primary
sources, study guides, images,
workshops, programs for teachers
and students, and much more. The
definitive Shakespeare website for
educators, historians and all lovers
of the Bard.

http://www.shakespeare.mit.edu.
The Complete Works of
William Shakespeare.
All complete scripts for *The
30-Minute Shakespeare* series were
originally downloaded from this site
before editing. Links to other internet
resources.

http://www.LoMonico.com/
Shakespeare-and-Media.htm
http://shakespeare-and-media
.wikispaces.com
Michael LoMonico is Senior
Consultant on National Education
for the Folger Shakespeare Library.
His *Seminar Shakespeare 2.0* offers a
wealth of information on how to use
exciting new approaches and online
resources for teaching Shakespeare.

http://www.freesound.org.
A collaborative database of sounds
and sound effects.

http://www.wordle.net.
A program for creating "word clouds"
from the text that you provide. The
clouds give greater prominence to
words that appear more frequently in
the source text.

http://www.opensourceshakespeare
.org.
This site has good searching capacity.

http://shakespeare.palomar.edu/
default.htm
Excellent links and searches

http://shakespeare.com/
Write like Shakespeare,
Poetry Machine, tag cloud

http://www.shakespeare-online.com/

http://www.bardweb.net/

http://www.rhymezone.com/
shakespeare/
Good searchable word and phrase
finder.
Or by lines:
http://www.rhymezone.com/
shakespeare/toplines/

http://shakespeare.mcgill.ca/
Shakespeare and Performance
research team

http://www.enotes.com/william-
shakespeare

Needless to say, the internet goes on and on with valuable Shakespeare resources.
The ones listed here are excellent starting points and will set you on your way in the
great adventure that is Shakespeare.

NICK NEWLIN has performed a comedy and variety act for international audiences for twenty-seven years. Since 1996, he has conducted an annual play directing residency affiliated with the Folger Shakespeare Library in Washington, D.C. Newlin received a BA with Honors from Harvard University in 1982 and an MA in Theater with an emphasis in Play Directing from the University of Maryland in 1996.

THE 30-MINUTE SHAKESPEARE

AS YOU LIKE IT
978-1-935550-06-8

**THE COMEDY
OF ERRORS**
978-1-935550-08-2

HAMLET
978-1-935550-24-2

HENRY IV, PART 1
978-1-935550-11-2

HENRY V
978-1-935550-38-9

JULIUS CAESAR
978-1-935550-29-7

KING LEAR
978-1-935550-09-9

**LOVE'S LABOR'S
LOST**
978-1-935550-07-5

MACBETH
978-1-935550-02-0

**A MIDSUMMER
NIGHT'S DREAM**
978-1-935550-00-6

**THE MERCHANT
OF VENICE**
978-1-935550-32-7

**THE MERRY WIVES
OF WINDSOR**
978-1-935550-05-1

**MUCH ADO ABOUT
NOTHING**
978-1-935550-03-7

OTHELLO
978-1-935550-10-5

RICHARD III
978-1-935550-39-6

ROMEO AND JULIET
978-1-935550-01-3

**THE TAMING OF THE
SHREW**
978-1-935550-33-4

THE TEMPEST
978-1-935550-28-0

TWELFTH NIGHT
978-1-935550-04-4

**THE TWO
GENTLEMEN OF
VERONA**
978-1-935550-25-9

**THE 30-MINUTE SHAKESPEARE
ANTHOLOGY**
978-1-935550-33-4

All plays $9.95, available in print and eBook editions in bookstores everywhere

*"A truly fun, emotional, and sometimes magical first experience . . . guided by
a sagacious, knowledgeable, and intuitive educator."* —Library Journal

PHOTOCOPYING AND PERFORMANCE RIGHTS

There is no royalty for performing any series of *The 30-Minute Shakespeare* in
a classroom or on a stage. The publisher hereby grants unlimited photocopy
permission for one series of performances to all acting groups that have
purchased the play. If a group stages a performance, please post a comment
and/or photo to our Facebook page; we'd love to hear about it!

Printed in the USA
CPSIA information can be obtained
at www.ICGtesting.com
JSHW012045140824
68134JS00034B/3262